NO LIE,
I ACTED LIKE A BEAST!

The Story of BEAUTY AND THE BEAST as Told by THE BEAST

by Nancy Loewen

illustrated by Cristian Bernardini

PICTURE WINDOW BOOKS
a capstone imprint

Special thanks to our adviser, Terry Flaherty, PhD, Professor of English,
Minnesota State University, Mankato, for his expertise.

Editor: Jill Kalz
Designer: Lori Bye
Art Director: Nathan Gassman
Production Specialist: Jennifer Walker
The illustrations in this book were created digitally.

Picture Window Books
1710 Roe Crest Drive
North Mankato, MN 56003
www.capstonepub.com

Library of Congress Cataloging-in-Publication Data
Loewen, Nancy, 1964–
No lie, I acted like a beast! : the story of Beauty and the Beast as told by the Beast / by
Nancy Loewen ; illustrated by Cristian Bernardini.
p. cm. — (The other side of the story)
ISBN 978-1-4048-7938-6 (library binding) — ISBN 978-1-4048-8083-2 (paperback)
[1. Actors—Fiction. 2. Humorous stories.] I. Bernardini, Cristian, 1975– ill. II. Title.
PZ7.L837No 2013
[E]—dc23
2012029562

Printed in the United States of America
in Stevens Point, Wisconsin.
052013   007391R

ROAR!

Argh!

Grrrr...

Yup, I've still got it.

I might not look like a beast anymore, but I can still act the part. Notice that I used the word "act"? Acting changed my life. It got me INTO trouble. It got me OUT of trouble. It even got me the girl of my dreams!

My name is Prince Elmer. If you believe the lies,
I was once a spoiled brat who refused to help
a poor old woman.

Here's the REAL story.

As a young prince, I was shy—so shy that I wouldn't even answer the phone. And if a pretty girl came around, forget it!

5

One day I read a notice in the newspaper.

THEATER AUDITIONS FOR

"THE THREE
BILLY GOATS GRUFF"

I decided then and there that I
was done being shy. I was going
to find my voice—as an actor!

Of course I wanted the best part in the play:
the evil troll who lives under the bridge. So I
practiced. And practiced.

I barked and hissed.

I growled as I brushed my teeth.

I slashed at the air with my fork.

On audition night, my head was so full of troll thoughts that at first I didn't notice the tug on my sleeve. It was a poor old woman asking for food.

"NO!" I roared. "I WON'T HELP YOU. GO AWAY!"

Then I remembered that I wasn't actually a troll. "Oh! I'm so sorry, I was just—"

But it was too late. Before my eyes, the old woman became an evil fairy. "Fool!" she cried. "You act like a beast. You shall BE a beast!"

"But you don't understand—"

"There is only one way to break this spell," the evil fairy said. "A woman must fall in love with you, in spite of your looks!" She snickered. "Like that's going to happen."

I must've fainted, because the next thing I knew,
I was in a strange castle. In the woods. Alone.

That was the worst time of my life. I was
hideous. Oh, sure, I had all sorts of fine things.
But I had no one to talk to.

10

To pass the time, I kept up my acting studies. In the garden I put on one-man shows for the birds and the butterflies.

11

Then came the stormy night that changed everything. A lost traveler took shelter in my castle. I remained hidden, but I made sure he had everything he needed. It felt awfully nice to have company.

The next morning, as he was leaving, he took a rose from the garden. That gave me an idea. Maybe I could trick him into coming back.

I'm not proud of what I did next, but it worked!

"IS THAT HOW YOU REWARD MY KINDNESS?" I roared. **"YOU WILL PAY WITH YOUR LIFE!"**

The man begged to say good-bye to his family.
He promised to return.

And he did—with his daughter named Beauty.
Beauty had vowed to take her father's place.
She felt responsible because she was the one
who'd asked for a rose.

For me, it was love at first sight. For
her—not so much. Who could blame
her? I had fur growing out of my
nostrils. And I smelled like a barn.

I went back to my shy ways, hiding behind drapes and ducking into closets. After a few days passed, Beauty figured out that I was more of a teddy bear than a beast. Imagine my delight when SHE started talking to ME.

We had a lot in common—including a love of good theater. I didn't have to do one-man shows anymore. I had a co-star! The more Beauty and I acted together, the more she got to know the real me.

One day, Beauty asked to leave the castle.
She wanted to visit her family.

"OK, but you'd better come back. I'll die without
you," I joked. And then my voice became serious.
"Really. If you leave me, I'll die."

Yes, it was a bit over the top. What can I say?
I'm an actor.

And with that,
she left.

When Beauty returned, she found me lying on the ground next to the rose bush. I tried not to breathe.

"Beast?" Beauty cried out. "Oh, no!"

Her tears poured onto my fur, but I didn't move.

"Oh, Beast, you're the ugliest creature I've ever seen. But—I can't help it, I love you! I do!"

And just like that, the spell was broken.
I got my Happily Ever After.

I was a prince again.

I married Beauty.

And together we've opened the Prince Elmer School of Beastly Good Acting.

You should take a class. It might change your life!

PRINCE ELMER SCHOOL OF BEASTLY GOOD ACTING

Think About It

Fairy tales have been around a long time, and they often have many different versions. What version of *Beauty and the Beast* do you know best? How is it different from this one? How is it the same?

How do you think this story would be different if it was told from another character's point of view? How about Beauty? Beauty's father?

Imagine living in a world in which fairies, witches, or other magical beings could appear at any moment. How would that affect your actions?

Prince Elmer was "in character" when he was rude to the old woman (who was actually an evil fairy). Have you ever been so lost in thought that you did something you really felt bad about? Even if Prince Elmer had been rude on purpose, do you think he would have deserved such punishment? Why or why not?

❧⚬❦❧⚬

Glossary

character—a person, animal, or creature in a story
point of view—a way of looking at something
version—a particular form of something

Read More

Dahl, Michael, retold by. *Beauty and the Beast: The Graphic Novel.* Mankato, Minn.: Stone Arch Books, 2009.

Jones, Christianne C., retelling by. *Beauty and the Beast.* Mankato, Minn.: Picture Window Books, 2011.

Sabuda, Robert. *Beauty & the Beast: A Pop-up Book of the Classic Fairy Tale.* Classic Collectible Pop-up. New York: Little Simon, 2010.

Internet Sites

FactHound offers a safe, fun way to find Internet sites related to this book. All of the sites on FactHound have been researched by our staff.

Here's all you do:
Visit *www.facthound.com*
Type in this code: 9781404879386

Look for all the books in the series:

Believe Me, Goldilocks Rocks!
Honestly, Red Riding Hood Was Rotten!
No Lie, I Acted Like a Beast!
Seriously, Cinderella Is SO Annoying!
Seriously, Snow White Was SO Forgetful!
Trust Me, Jack's Beanstalk Stinks!

Super-cool stuff! Check out projects, games and lots more at **www.capstonekids.com**